THE RED HERRING BOOK OF
FOOD FACTS

By the same author

Two Points East - A View Of Maritime Norfolk

Curlew Coast - Diversions on Maritime Suffolk

Published by Red Herring Publishing

Judith Ellis 2020

www.thebookstudio.co.uk

ISBN 978-1-9997839-4-5

Cover design by **studio medlikova**

Illustrations by Janine Pope

janine@mudrabbit.co.uk

Printed and bound in the UK by Barnwell Print

All profits to be donated to the Trussell Trust supporting the food banks

Judith Ellis

THE RED HERRING BOOK OF
FOOD FACTS

with illustrations by

Janine Pope

and a few red herrings......

CONTENTS

INTRODUCTION

With a background in science (I practised as a veterinary surgeon for many years) and an interest in food, like many people I have been fascinated by the relatively recent revelations on the importance of the bacteria and other micro-organisms in our gut and their enormous influence not only on our physical health, but also on our wellbeing and mental health.

Most of us have become much more aware of health problems connected with different foods, from gluten and lactose intolerance to IBS. I have been surprised to find that many of my friends have only a hazy idea of how their bodies work and it is in response to this that I thought it would be useful to write a short guide to help navigate a way through the mass of, often conflicting, information that comes at us through the internet and other media.

Science sometimes gets a bad name when its guidelines for healthy eating seem to suddenly change. The consumption of fat, for instance, and its connection with blood cholesterol is just one of these. But no scientific finding is ever the last word on anything - it will always be work in progress and its findings are only valid until another step forward is taken in our understanding of the complex workings of our world.

How concerned should we be about diet?

Most of us choose to eat some healthy foods and some which may not be, food after all is a pleasure and eating with family and friends is an important form of social interaction. Eating a pastry or a sausage is never going to kill you, but eating processed food routinely may increase one of your risk factors for cancer, diabetes and cardiovascular disease. These risk factors will be different from person to person, but if we are making choices it is better, I think, that those choices should be informed ones.

This book has several aims.

To provide a brief reminder of how our bodies process the food we eat and to try to bring some clarity to the ever-increasing and baffling array of foods which are now available in the supermarkets.

The relatively recent discoveries being made about the importance of the gut biome has brought the public's attention to the benefits of healthy eating, but with information overload on the internet, it is sometimes hard to know how much of it you can trust.

I hope it will prove useful as a reference guide for anyone wanting to be better informed about the way their bodies work and the foods that they are buying. I hope that it will arm the unwary with enough knowledge not to be taken in by some of the misleading claims of the food industry, which are often designed to give the impression that their products are healthier than they really are; and finally the profits from every copy sold will be donated to the food banks.

We will start with the supermarkets.

1 NAVIGATING THE SUPERMARKET

It is easy to be taken in by the marketing of foods. Recognising the demand for a better diet, the food industry introduce key words onto their labels, assuming that you will take them at face value. It is a way of getting you to think that their product is healthier than other foods. For example vegetable crisps contain just as much fat as potato crisps. Look out for the following words:

Healthy Most food is 'healthy' it is usually what has been either added to it or taken away that is the problem.

Organic If it has been grown in a country where corruption is not endemic you can be reasonably sure it really has been grown without herbicides and pesticides. But bear in mind that there are some countries where organic verification certificates can be bought, for the right price.

Organic food can taste better and that is likely to be because it is of a different variety from those which are grown for mass production, where it is their packaging and keeping qualities that are valued more than taste.

Farm fresh Most food is grown on farms, including intensive farms where the animals may be kept confined for most of the time.

The chicken and the egg

Free range Free-range hens have to have access to outdoors but they are often in closely packed barns and do not spend much time outside, although that does remain a choice for them. A bird scraping around outside eating vegetation and insects will naturally produce a yolk that is a deep yellow in colour, although this can also be achieved by adding beta-carotene to the food.

Barn range is much better than the old, and now illegal, system of caged birds, but they are still confined in a barn with no access to the outside.

Fats, superfoods and sugars

Superfood This does not mean very much. All nuts, seeds, berries etc contain vitamins and trace elements. Some may contain a bit more than others but that does not really make them into 'superfoods'.

Reduced fat This is not the same as low in fat. The legal requirement is that it should be reduced by a minimum of 25%, so a product with 40% fat, such as most cheeses, will count as reduced if the level drops to 30%; still quite high.

Salads Watch for the dressing, as prepared salads usually have dressings with large quantities of salt, sugar and oil. An example of a healthy food source transformed into something else completely.

Sugar-free This is a trap for the unwary. Honey, agave syrup, date syrup and every other kind of sweet syrup is just sucrose and fructose from a source other than sugar-cane or sugar-beet. Sucrose and fructose are quickly broken down to glucose on digestion and it makes no difference as to which source it came from. It is dishonest to say that something made with date or agave syrup is sugar-free. The darker the sugar the less it has been refined. These sugars may contain traces of minerals and their advantage is to add interesting flavours and textures for baking - they are not any healthier. Golden syrup, treacle, molasses, muscovado and other brown sugars all represent different stages in the refining process.

Sweeteners contain very few calories but they have the same effect on insulin production as sugar does.

The use by date on the egg box is 4 weeks after the date they were laid. The best before date is 3 weeks after laying.

Fruit juices and smoothies These contain really large amounts of sugar. You would not want to eat your way through five or six oranges because they would fill you up with fibre before you got to the last one, but you can easily consume the same amount of sugar that they contain in just one glassful.

Sourdough Supermarket sourdough bread has a better texture and flavour than the other supermarket breads but it has not had the slow rise using the mix of old varieties of yeast that the artisan bakers use. It is this slow rise that makes the bread much more digestible. Supermarkets value speed of production over nutritional value.

Processed meats Hams, bacon, sausages, chorizo and salami all contain salt, nitrites and nitrates which are used as preservatives. These are implicated in the development of bowel cancer - if you are genetically susceptible, nitrites may trigger it off. Nitrites, usually in the form of saltpetre, have traditionally been used to produce the pink colouration which we are used to (they do this by reacting with haemoglobin in the blood). But there are companies now that sell nitrite-free salami, sausages and bacon. Ask your butcher if he uses nitrites and nitrates when he makes his sausages.

.

Nitrates or nitrites? - the technical bit

Nitrates and nitrites are not in themselves harmful, it is the changes they undergo in your body that converts them into potentially harmful chemicals.

Nitrates convert to nitrites in your mouth as they mix with saliva. The nitrites then react with proteins, in the presence of the acids found in the stomach, where they are converted to the carcinogenic chemical *nitrosamine*.

You can tell a free-range chicken by the length of its leg bones. A caged bird grows very fast and they are usually killed at 6 weeks. A bird reared outdoors takes longer to grow to an equivalent size so, being older, its leg bones will be longer.

2 THE BASICS - A Reminder

HOW THE DIGESTIVE SYSTEM WORKS

When food is swallowed it first enters the **stomach** where it mixes with the stomach acids and is churned up into a porridge-like substance called *chyle*.

The chyle then makes its way through to the **small intestine** where it mixes with enzymes, from the **pancreas,** and with bile salts, from the **liver**. The enzymes break everything down further into nutrients that can then be absorbed through the lining of the intestine. There are relatively few bacteria in this part of the gut and it is here where most of the nutrients are absorbed. Food spends roughly three to five hours in the small intestine.

It then continues its journey into the **large intestine**, also called the colon, passing the appendix on its way. It is here in the colon where most of the gut bacteria, yeasts and fungi live - our very own **microbiome.**

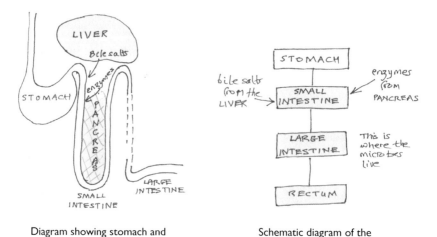

Diagram showing stomach and
small intestine

Schematic diagram of the
digestive system

Enter the microbiome

The discovery of the importance of the microbiome is relatively new and one of the most fascinating advances in the understanding of our health. It appears that the healthiest people are those who have the most diverse number of species of micro-organisms in their gut. Someone on the average western diet will have around 20,000 different species, while a member of a tribe of hunter-gatherers may have as many as 50,000. The more diverse the diet the more diverse the microbiome will be.

The power of the microbe - who is in charge round here?

Microbes are able to manipulate what we want to eat. The lining of the gut contains neurones which connect to the brain, and if you have a lot of the sort of bacteria that are only interested in devouring sugar, they will send a message to your brain via these neurones making you want to eat more of it. The more they multiply, the greater the numbers of sugar-demanding microbes there will be to press you to consume more in an ever-increasing spiral. It seems that those cravings are actually being directed by the microbes.

It is now becoming easier to see why a diet made up of only a few different foods is going to encourage only a few different types of microbe, so many of the other important ones will not get enough nourishment to sustain enough numbers to contribute to your health.

The rise and fall of Akkermansia

One particular microbe, bearing the rather striking name of *Akkermansia*, is very particular about what it needs to eat and chooses to eat only the mucus which is found on the surface of the gut lining. This means it can only feed when the gut is empty. A fast of at least twelve hours each day will ensure this state can be reached, so a gap of at least twelve hours between your evening meal and your breakfast will conveniently satisfy both you and your very demanding bacteria.

The Immune System

The immune system works day and night to keep everything functioning smoothly. It has *phage* cells which hoover up and destroy anything which should not be there such as invading bacteria and any cells of your own which have become cancerous. The gut microbes seem to play some role in briefing the immune system on what should be attacked and what should be left alone. A healthy system functioning well gives you no indication of how hard it is constantly working to keep everything in order.

Homeostasis is the word used to describe the tendency of a system to maintain its stability, and our bodies manage to achieve this most of the time. But look beneath the surface and the body is a battleground of competing interests between the home team of resident microbes, your own immune cells and anything else passing by in the bloodstream. When you stop to think of how many times our cells divide and mutate over a lifetime, it is pretty amazing that most rogue cells are picked up and dealt with.

But it is all too easy for some of our phages to be misdirected in their enthusiasm for destruction and they will sometimes turn on our body's own cells causing what we call an *auto-immune* disease. The whole system is so interconnected and immensely complex that it is surprising that cancer and auto-immune disorders are not more common than they are.

Food takes between twenty-four and forty-eight hours to make its journey from one end to the other.

THE COMPONENTS OF FOOD

Carbohydrates

These are starches and sugars which are all ultimately broken down by the enzyme *amylase* which makes them into glucose, the high octane fuel on which our bodies run. There two basic types of carbs.

Simple carbohydrates are the sugars *sucrose,* found in sugar-cane and sugar-beet, *fructose* found in fruit and *lactose* found in milk.

Foods which are simple carbohydrates are **honey, white and brown sugars and all syrups.**

Complex carbohydrates are those found in grains, starchy vegetables and pulses. These complex ones generally take a lot more breaking down to convert them into glucose.

They are found in **grains** and so are in **bread, pasta and breakfast cereals, starchy fruit and vegetables** such as **potatoes, all the root vegetables, bananas, apples, pears etc and pulses** such as **lentils and beans.**

Any glucose not needed for immediate use is stored in the liver (in the form of *glycogen*), or as body fat.

The names of the different sugars all end in the suffix *..ose,* and the names of the enzymes all end in *....ase.*

Proteins

The proteins which we need are made up of about twenty different *amino acids*, the building blocks of protein, and if we do not get all of them in our diet we will develop signs of disease. Meat and dairy products all contain the complete range, but not all of the plant proteins do. The only exceptions to this are **quinoa, buckwheat and amaranth**.

This means that a vegetarian diet needs to have protein from more than one source to ensure all twenty amino acids are present. As vegans do not eat eggs or dairy products they need to pay particular attention to this.

Interestingly, dishes from the traditional plant-based diets of the East such as hummus (made from sesame seeds and chickpeas) and various pulses served with rice and so on, will all naturally contain the full range because of the combinations they are in.

Foods high in protein are **meat, eggs, nuts, seeds, beans, lentils, grains such as oats and quinoa, peas and tofu(made from soya beans).**

Fats

Attitude to fats has changed a lot in recent years. Fat is essential to life; it is not only needed for maintaining every system in the body from our brains to our skin, but we cannot absorb some of the vitamins without it. Fats give us the feeling of being full faster and for longer than carbohydrates will and it is the way we store excess food. Anything with a high fat content usually tastes fantastic.

Fat is broken down into smaller units called *lipids* by the enzyme *lipase* in the small intestine. From there they enter the *lymphatic system,* a network of tubes running alongside the blood vessels, which all meet up at a very large tube (the *Ductus thoracicus*) which discharges the lipids directly into the blood in the heart. The lipids are now in the bloodstream where some of them can contribute to the clogging up of our arteries, before eventually arriving in the liver. The job of the liver is to detoxify any 'bad' fats and sort out storage for those not needed for immediate use either within the liver itself or in the tissues as body fat.

What are the different types of fat?

Fats can be either *saturated* or *unsaturated,* and animal fats and plant oils all contain both in varying proportions. Animal fats are high in saturated fat, which makes them solid like the fat on meat, and the plant oils are high in **un**saturated fat which makes them liquid. The exception to this is coconut oil which is high in saturated fat and so is solid like butter.

Saturated fats

It used to be thought that saturated fat contributed to high LDL cholesterol, the 'bad' cholesterol, but all this is currently under review.

Animal fats contain a much larger proportion of a fatty acid called *arachidonic acid* than do the vegetable fats and this is responsible for producing a neurotransmitter involved in inflammation. Vegetable oils on the other hand have a much higher proportion of **anti-**inflammatory fatty acids and these will help to reduce inflammation.

Foods high in saturated fats are **butter, lard, cheese, sausages and the fat on meat.** Also, unusually for a plant fat, **coconut oil.**

Unsaturated fats

These fats can be **mono-unsaturated** or **poly-unsaturated** and are usually in liquid form as oils. Both these fats are anti-inflammatory and that could be one of the reasons why a plant-based diet can reduce the symptoms of some inflammatory diseases like arthritis. But all unsaturated fats are not equal. The polyunsaturated ones are not chemically stable at high temperatures and some of them are actually harmful when heated or exposed to air or sunlight. (See the section on cooking oils p 32).

Fish oils are also high in unsaturated fats and contain particularly large amounts of omega-3 and omega-6 fatty acids. Evening primrose and starflower oils are also very good sources for this (vegans take note).

Foods high in unsaturated fat are **nuts, seeds, avocados, olives, vegetable oils, eggs, oily fish, cheese** and **dark chocolate!**

 The higher the fat content of any food, the more palatable it will be and the longer food will remain in your stomach.

Vitamins

Vitamins A D E and K can only be absorbed with fat (they are called the fat soluble vitamins) and are all stored by the body for use when needed. If you do not have enough fat in your diet, or your body cannot digest fat, you will not be able to absorb these vitamins.

The water soluble vitamins on the other hand are absorbed on a need-only basis and any amount of these vitamins you take on board above your daily requirements will be simply excreted through the kidneys. These are the B vitamins, and vitamin C. They cannot be stored in the body so do need to be eaten every day. This means there is not a lot of point in taking supplements of these vitamins if you are already eating a balanced diet. **Vitamin B12** however does not occur in plants, and is only found in **meat, eggs, and dairy products**.

 Vegans need to take a B12 supplement.

Minerals

These are also called trace elements, and they are not absorbed well on their own so if you are taking a supplement it is much better to take it as part of a meal. There can be many factors causing mineral deficiencies among which are a restricted diet such as one which excludes both meat and dairy products; this vegan diet is very low in iron, zinc, calcium and phosphorus.

Many minerals are only absorbed in the right balance with other minerals. Calcium and phosphorus are linked in such a way so that too much of one will lead to not enough of the other being absorbed. To add to the general complication, both calcium and phosphorus also need the presence of Vitamin D if they are going to be absorbed at all.

The good news is that we can manufacture some of our own Vitamin D using sunlight on the skin. The bad news is that we do not get much exposure to sunlight in the winter, and when the sun actually does come out we now tend to slap on ever more efficient sunblocking creams. Vitamin D levels can become very low for those living in a northern climate.

Vegetarians may also become low on iron and zinc, as meat still remains the best source for both of these. Plant based milks are usually fortified with Vitamin D as well as calcium.

Foods high in **calcium** are **dairy products, leafy vegetables and those plant milks which have been fortified.**

Foods high in **iron** are **meat, beans, nuts, wholegrains and leafy vegetables.**

Foods high in **zinc** are **meat, shellfish and dairy foods.**

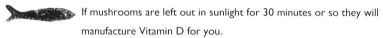 If mushrooms are left out in sunlight for 30 minutes or so they will manufacture Vitamin D for you.

Fibre

There are two sorts of fibre, *soluble* and *insoluble* and to add to the confusion some of these are referred to as being prebiotic as well. Most fibre-rich foods actually contain both sorts in varying proportions. Insoluble fibre is a bulking agent, while water soluble fibre keeps everything in the gut soft.

Prebiotic fibre

This sort of fibre is essential for feeding the good gut bacteria, the 'bad' bacteria do not use it, and if your diet contains a lot of prebiotic fibre, it will promote the growth of the good bacteria in your gut. And the more of them the better.

Foods high in prebiotic fibre are plants from the onion family - **leeks, onions and garlic, endives, both sorts of artichokes, salsify, oats, almonds, flaxseeds, pulses and lentils, apples and bananas.**

The prebiotic fibre *inulin*, occurs in particularly high amounts in **kiwi fruit,** and it can be bought over the counter as a white powder. The bacteria *Bifidobacteria* and *Lactobacillus* love to consume this, and it is sometimes added to processed food as a sweetener.

Resistant and unresistant starch

The starches in cooked pasta, white rice and potato do not have any accompanying fibre and so they are very quickly absorbed and converted into glucose, that is they have a high glycaemic index. But a very interesting thing happens when cooked rice, pasta or potato become cold; the previously unresistant starch converts itself into resistant starch. It has converted itself into prebiotic fibre and the faster the pasta or rice is cooled down the more efficient the conversion. When these foods are re-heated the starch remains in this resistant form making it a very good idea to cook pasta and rice and potatoes ahead of time for reheating later when needed.

Glycaemic index

This refers to the speed at which carbohydrates are absorbed and converted into glucose. A carbohydrate food source with very little fibre, such as white bread, white rice, sugary foods and anything made with white flour and starches have a high glycaemic index. They will give you a quick 'sugar rush' followed by an equally fast drop in blood glucose.

Carbohydrates with a high fibre content such as oats and other wholegrains (and their flours), will all have a low glycaemic index giving a much slower absorption and conversion to glucose. This sustains a steadier level of glucose in the blood for longer and is why porridge makes a more sustaining breakfast than a packeted sugary cereal.

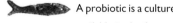 A probiotic is a culture of different bacteria such as live yoghurt or kefir. Also available in the form of capsules.

What about antinutrients?

Nuts, seeds, pulses and grains are all surrounded with a coating containing *phytates* (also called phytic acid) in variable amounts. These are commonly known as *antinutrients* as they will bind with minerals such as calcium, phosphorus, iron and zinc, and prevent them from being absorbed. They also seem to cause a lot of anxiety amongst wholefood afficianados, who will go to great lengths to remove them. But phytates will only reduce your absorption of minerals in the food that contains them, so if you eat some almonds, the phytates in them will simply prevent you from absorbing the minerals in the almonds, not from the whole meal.

Vitamin C (aka *ascorbic acid,*) will break down phytates, so that eating foods rich in Vitamin C at the same time will counteract antinutrients, as will fermenting, sprouting or soaking the grains for a few hours prior to using them. Yoghurt naturally contains phytase producing bacteria too. You will find websites giving all sorts of advice on this, even recommending that flour should be soaked before using it, but with a varied and balanced diet this is really not necessary.

Once again it is interesting to note that many of the traditional Eastern dishes eaten with rice or other grains will contain also yoghurt or fruit, thereby adding fermenting bacteria or vitamin C to the dish.

The good news

You don't really have to remember any of this, it is simply an explanation of why the best diet is one that contains a wide variety of different foods. It will then all just take care of itself, antinutrients included.

If you exercise immediately after eating your body will use the quickly available glucose already in your blood. If you need to lose weight it might be better to exercise before eating, thereby making your body use its own fat reserves.

3 WHEN THINGS GO WRONG

There seem to be many more people now with food issues, the most common seeming to be intolerances to gluten and to lactose. There have also been some high profile cases recently of people dying from being exposed to a particular food they are allergic to.

What is the difference between an allergy, an intolerance and a food poisoning?

An allergic reaction is immediate, sudden in onset and produces acute symptoms such as a rash or swellings, which can be potentially dangerous if the result is to block the airways. We have all become much more aware now of children developing allergies to nuts and to milk.

In some cases an allergic reaction can escalate into *anaphylactic shock* - a catastrophic reaction by the body which is fatal unless treated immediately.

An intolerance to a food produces less acute symptoms, usually associated with the gut - bloating, discomfort, pain, diarrhoea or constipation etc. It can be hard to work out which particular food is causing the problem without a sustained and systematic elimination of foods one at a time.

Food poisoning is usually caused by the bacteria *Campylobacter, Salmonella* or *E.coli*, and the symptoms of diarrhoea and vomiting will occur within a few hours of eating the contaminated food.

These bacteria will all be killed by cooking, but food poisoning is often due to cross-contamination in the kitchen, where raw meat has been prepared in the same place as food ready to eat, or when the same implements have been used. Chickens reared intensively are often contaminated with one of these bacteria. The recent and ongoing controversy of US chlorinated chicken relates to this problem. In the UK our chickens are produced under strict regulations concerning the numbers of fowl which can be kept together, the stocking density. Hens are no longer reared jammed in together in battery cages and there are regulations about the amount of space per bird. This is all about welfare of the birds, but the decreased stocking density also reduces the spread of bacteria. In the United States, they do not have the high standards of welfare that we have in the UK and the higher incidence of bacteria which result, is dealt with by washing the chicken carcasses with chlorinated water. There are differing opinions on the efficacy of the chorine or of the alternative lactic acid as a disinfectant, but the more important issue surely must be the inhumane methods of rearing the birds in the first place.

Food poisoning can also be caused by a **toxin**, which is a poison produced by a bacterium such as E.coli or Clostridium. If a toxin is present in the food the effect will be much more rapid. An example of this would be botulism or an E.coli toxin from a shellfish.

 Campylobacter is frequently carried by wild birds. Worth remembering when filling or cleaning birdfeeders.

INTOLERANCE TO GLUTEN

This does seem to be becoming more common. Gluten is a protein found in wheat and to a lesser extent in barley and rye. In baking, the raising agents such as baking powder or yeast produce air bubbles which become trapped in the strands of gluten making the mix into an airy structure. The gluten retains this expanded structure when it is cooked giving us light well-risen cakes and breads.

Over the last hundred years as food production became more industrial, varieties of wheat have been bred to contain more and more gluten, to satisfy our desire for white bread and light cakes. They have also been bred to have a looser connection between the husk and the grain itself, making it even easier to refine white flour. This means that our modern flours have more gluten and less fibre than those used in the past. The other big change in the baking industry has been to develop a single variety of yeast which produces a fast fermentation and therefore a much speedier production of factory produced bread.

The traditional way of making a yeast-risen dough was by allowing the natural yeasts in the air and on the grain itself to develop over a period of several days. Instead of using our modern monoculture of yeast, some of this starter, made of dough and natural yeasts, was kept back to use with the next batch of bread. This is what we now call the sourdough method - a mixture of different yeasts working slowly over many hours, allowing the flour to develop complex flavours and breaking down some of the gluten.

Ever since Man started farming 12,000 years ago, we have been cultivating wheat above all other grains and the western diet has remained a wheat-based one.

Our exposure to foods with a high gluten content has escalated in recent years as the food industry persuades us to eat more and more breads, cakes and pastries.

Many people with an intolerance find they can eat a certain amount of sourdough bread because of its reduced gluten content.

Coeliac disorder is much more serious than gluten intolerance. It can come on at any stage in life and is a disease of the small intestine. If the smallest amount of gluten enters the small intestine, it triggers antibodies which destroy the intestinal lining through which all food is absorbed. An undiagnosed coeliac sufferer will be unable to digest very much food which leads to weight loss and malnutrition.

If gluten is removed completely from the diet, the intestinal lining will regenerate and start to function normally. It is important for a coeliac sufferer that not a trace of gluten is allowed in and coeliacs will have to prepare food in a different area in the kitchen to avoid cross-contamination with wheat flour or crumbs. They will even need to use a separate toaster. Many processed foods, ready meals etc contain small amounts of gluten, and to be certified gluten-free it has to be guaranteed that the mill through which the flour was made had not previously milled a product which did contain gluten. Oats, which do not naturally contain gluten anyway, can only be sold as gluten-free if the mill has not previously been used for wheat.

> **Foods made from wheat**
> -Couscous
> -Bulghur
> -Semolina
> -Freekah
> -Pasta
> -Bread
> -Pastry
> -Most cakes

INTOLERANCE TO LACTOSE

Lactose is the sugar found in milk and we need the enzyme lactase to break it down into glucose. But some people stop producing lactase later in life and so become unable to digest lactose leading to lactose intolerance. The symptoms of lactose intolerance are much the same as for gluten intolerance and largely relate to the gut, with bloating, discomfort, and diarrhoea being common signs.

Lactose is a sugar present in milk, which, like wheat, seems to have become another common component of the western diet to the extent that a huge variety of milk based foods can be found in the dairy section of every supermarket. With the ever-increasing availability of foods from different parts of the world, there is a bewildering choice of dairy foods now. (See Chapter Five on dairy products)

 The suffix ....*itis* means inflammation. So arth*itis* is inflammation of the joints, col*itis* is inflammation of the colon etc.

4 GOING GLUTEN FREE

No-one would choose to go gluten free. Most of the readily available baked foods are based on wheat and unless it states otherwise most rye breads contain some wheat flour. Unless you are prepared to cook for yourself, a gluten free diet is not a very healthy one. There are several reasons for this.

Rice, beware the hidden arsenic

Most of the prepared GF foods are made with white rice flour and rice cakes seem to fill up a large amount of shelf space in the supermarkets now. Rice is a grain that contains very small amounts of arsenic - the rice plant has an increased tendency to absorb this, as well as other trace elements, from the soil. Eaten as a part of one's diet this is of no significance at all, but if you are eating manufactured baked foods regularly, you will be consuming large amounts of rice flour and over a number of years, you will be exposing yourself to rather more arsenic than might be good for you.

Where is the fibre?

Most baked goods such as breads, pastries and cakes are based on potato or tapioca starch and white rice flour. Starch is a carbohydrate of little nutritional value and white rice flour has no fibre either. Even brown GF bread will be made largely from starch with some added wholegrain flour or seeds, for flavour. Some of them are a very suspicious orangey shade of brown which suggests they may be artificially coloured with caramelised sugar.

Some gluten traps

It is not always apparent which foods are based on wheat, barley or rye. Here are a few of the common ones.

Spelt is a variety of wheat which has less gluten than most wheat flours and can sometimes be tolerated by people with a gluten intolerance, but it is still wheat and still contains gluten.

Barley and rye both contain gluten.

All the following foods are made from wheat.

- **Semolina** is coarsely ground durum wheat, the hard wheat grown for strong bread flour.
- **Couscous** is made from semolina which has been steamed and tossed with wheat flour to make it into tiny balls.
- **Bulghur** is cracked durum wheat which has been partially cooked by boiling.
- **Freekah** is roasted green durum wheat. It is sometimes sprouted.
- **Pasta** is also made from wheat - look for buckwheat pasta instead.
- **Noodles** just like spaghetti, are made from wheat flour. (The rice noodles found in southern Chinese cooking are, unsurprisingly, made from rice flour and so do not contain gluten).
- **Bread, cakes and pastry.**
- **Sauces** thickened with wheat flour. (cornflour is made from maize, so does not contain gluten).
- Most **beers** are made from malted wheat or barley.

If you are coeliac, rather than just gluten intolerant you will have to read the list of contents of processed food very carefully indeed. Even Marmite contains small amounts of barley.

Oats which are not certified gluten free may be contaminated with a little wheat due either to the harvested oats mixing with some wheat grain in the field, or wheat flour residues left in the mill from a previous grinding.

The good news

- Spirits like whisky, vodka, brandy etc are distilled so they do not contain any gluten.

- Pasta made from buckwheat or from bean flours taste very good.

- Supermarket GF bread may be a disappointment but you can always use it to make breadcrumbs for cooking.

- Lentil or buckwheat cakes may resemble those polystyrene flotation devices which are sold as rice cakes, but they do actually taste rather good.

- Oats do not contain gluten, although some gluten intolerant people cannot handle the related protein called *avenin* which is found in oats.

- Quinoa is a good rice substitute. Grind it to make flour, soak it to make a crunchy topping for salads, or cook it instead of rice. If you bake it in the oven with some water it will not come out quite as wet as when it is boiled. It will benefit from toasting in the oven or some sort of flavour adding to it such as harissa, spices, herbs etc.

- There are many culinary adventures to be had in trying out things from wholefood shops.

 Soya contains high levels of phyto-oestrogens which will bind calcium preventing it from being absorbed. Bear it in mind if you are not getting calcium from dairy foods either.

5   DAIRY PRODUCTS - A Guide for the Perplexed

These are all made from milk and include an increasing variety of foods from cheese and fromage frais, to quark and yoghurt. Let's have a look at the cheeses first.

CHEESES

Cheese is made by curdling milk with either an acid, such as lemon juice or vinegar, or fermenting bacteria, such as *Lactobacillus*. Curdling the milk, separates the solid curds from the watery whey.

The **curd** contains all of the fat and the protein *casein,* while the **whey** contains the proteins *albumen* and *globulin* and all of the lactose.

Lactose

If the curdling is done by the fermentation method, the bacteria that have been added to the milk, will continue to grow, feeding on the lactose and gradually gobbling it up as time goes on. This means that cheeses made with bacteria will contain less lactose than those which use acid; and it also follows that the older the cheese the less lactose it will contain.

Fat

If the cheese has been made with skimmed milk then it will clearly be much lower in fat than one made with whole milk. Some cheeses can also be made with reduced-fat milk thereby adding another layer of complexity to navigating the dairy counter. The flavour of cheese is largely carried in the fat it contains which is why manufacturers will often add sugar to their reduced fat cheeses and yoghurts in order to improve the flavour.

Cottage cheese is made by curdling milk with an acid. The whey is then drained off, taking a lot of the lactose with it, leaving the casein-rich curds. This makes cottage cheese high in protein and low in both fat and lactose. It is generally about 4% fat unless made from skimmed milk.

Quark is made in a similar way to cottage cheese but it is curdled using bacteria rather than an acid. It is usually made from skimmed milk, so it is low in fat and as the whey containing the lactose is drained off, it will be low in lactose as well. It is generally 0.2% fat.

Feta is made from sheep or goat's milk curdled with bacteria. The whey is separated and drained off, and the curds aged for two months before salting it in brine. The bacteria continues to break down the lactose, so the older the feta the less lactose it will contain. It is generally about 20% fat.

Ricotta is made by heating the whey left over from other cheesemaking, so it remains high in lactose, but it does also contain the proteins albumen and globulin. It is generally about 8% fat.

Soft cheeses These are young cheeses which have not matured long enough for much reduction of lactose by the lactose-consuming bacteria.

On the fat stakes, generally Brie is about 29% , soft goats cheese 26% , and Camembert 23%. They will of course all be high in lactose.

Fromage Frais is another soft young cheese made by fermenting milk with bacteria. It will still contain lactose and its fat content depends on whether it has been made from skimmed or whole milk.

Mascarpone is made with acid so remains high in lactose. It is also very high in fat, anywhere between 45 - 75%.

Cream cheese is again made with acid and often has stabilisers added to give it a creamy texture. It varies widely in fat content.

Hard cheeses are made by curdling milk with bacteria and separating off the lactose-containing whey.

The older the cheese the less lactose as the bacteria continue to use it up. Edam is about 29% fat, Parmesan 30% and Cheddar and Stilton both about 35%,
YOGHURTS

These are made from fermenting milk with bacteria so are all reduced in lactose.

Skyr This Icelandic yoghurt is made from skimmed milk and so is naturally low in fat. It is first fermented with bacteria and then a small amount of rennet added to curdle it, allowing some of the whey to be strained off, before it is finally filtered. Skyr yoghurt is low in both lactose and fat.

Full fat yoghurt is strained to reduce the whey content making it thicker and concentrating the casein and fats as well as reducing the lactose.

Labneh This is the strained yoghurt used in the Middle East and can be made by leaving yoghurt to drain more of its lactose-containing whey overnight in a sieve.

Kefir is a type of yoghurt that has been fermented with a much greater variety of bacteria.

Alpro yoghurt is made from soya so has no lactose at all.

CREAMS high lactose

Sour cream, and creme fraiche are made by fermenting with bacteria, like the soft cheeses and yoghurts but starting with cream not milk. The fat content varies as sometimes more fat is added for texture and flavour.

Sour cream usually has thickeners added to it such as gelatine or rennet and is usually 20% fat.

Creme fraiche is naturally thick due to the longer culturing time. It is usually 30% fat.

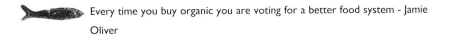 Every time you buy organic you are voting for a better food system - Jamie Oliver

6 THE COMPLICATED WORLD OF COOKING OILS *Source : Michael Moseley*

As if all that is not enough, it now seems that we should have to start thinking about which cooking oils are the safest to use.

The reason for this is that plant oils will deteriorate when subjected to high temperatures, subsequently becoming harmful. There is a lot of information on the internet, and in the newer cookery books, offering advice on this subject, giving lists of the 'smoke points' of various oils and then making conflicting statements about how good or bad they are for you.

Like a lot of things in life this is rarely as simple as you would like it to be, so we need to delve into a little into a bit of science.

All fats and oils are made up of three types of fat.

- **Saturated fat** - these are found in large amounts in animal fats and coconut oil, and in smaller amounts in other plant oils.

- **Monounsaturated** and **polyunsaturated fats** - both of these are found in large amounts in plants, with the notable exception of coconut oil, and only small amounts are found in animal fats.

Aldehydes - polyunsaturated fat's hidden weapon

When exposed to light, or when heated, polyunsaturated fats will oxidise and start to release harmful chemicals called *aldehydes* (sometimes referred to as 'free radicals') and these are linked to the inflammation that underlies heart disease and cancer. Oxidisation also happens at room temperature, albeit very slowly, and that is what has happened when a fat has gone rancid. As you heat an oil up the oxidisation speeds up too, reaching its peak at its 'smoke point', that is the point at which you can see smoke arising from the pan and the smoke alarm goes off.....

So far, so straightforward, and you could conclude at this point that you just need to know which oils have a high smoke point, thereby rendering them safe to use for moderate temperature frying , and all will be clear. Or is it? Although all refined oils have quite a high a smoke point (mostly well above 190C), there is always going to be a but.

What have the manufacturers done to the oil before it enters your kitchen? The simplest way of extracting oil from plants is to mechanically press the olives, seeds or whatever the chosen plant is, and this is called cold-pressing. But some oils at this stage will have a particularly strong taste so these are often then refined using heat, steam or solvents in order to 'deodorise' them. We have already seen that heating an oil will cause the polysaturates in it to oxidise and release harmful aldehydes. This means that refined oils will already contain the harmful aldehydes before they have even hit the supermarket shelves. Oils refined by heating tend to have higher smoke points than the unrefined ones, but the very process of refining them will already have produced the aldehydes you are trying to avoid.

So there has to be some sort of trade-off. Rather than leaving this decision to one of the many websites or cookery books, which often give conflicting advice, the table on the next page allows you to see the relative pros and cons of some of the different oils enabling you to make an informed decision yourself.

Table showing the polyunsaturated fat content of some cooking oils.

oil	% polyunsat. fat	% monounsat. fat	% saturated fat
sunflower	65	20	10
corn	54	27	12
sesame	41	40	14
groundnut	30	50	20
cold pressed rapeseed	28	63	7
extra virgin olive	10	76	14
goose fat	11	56	27
lard	11	45	39
butter	3	21	51
coconut	2	6	86

Note the very high polyunsaturate content of sunflower and corn oils - not good oils to be heating up at all.

Linseed is another name for flaxseed.

To summarise then, there are three things to consider when choosing an oil

1.The higher the percentage of polyunsaturate an oil contains, the more aldehydes it will develop when heated.

2. If it has been refined using heat it will already contain aldehydes.

3. Much is often made of the smoke point of an oil (the temperature at which it will be releasing the most aldehydes). But this is never written on the label, and taken on its own it is not particularly helpful.

Based on all this information it would seem that the animal fats such as butter and lard, coconut oil and cold-pressed extra virgin olive oil would be the safest to use for cooking, as they are all very low in polyunsaturates.

Cold-pressed rapeseed and groundnut oils would be the next safest.

Sesame, corn and sunflower oils are best not used for cooking at all.

Finally, to slow down their oxidisation, all cooking oils should be kept cool, in a cupboard away from light, and they should be replaced every so often.

The good news

All cold-pressed oils are safe to use for dressings or for drizzling on food *after* cooking.

Hydrogenated fats are vegetable oils which have had hydrogen pumped through them to make the oil go solid, (margarine is a good example of this). The hydrogenation produces *trans-fats* which are known to be harmful. They are commonly found in manufactured baked goods such as biscuits and cakes.

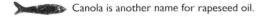 Canola is another name for rapeseed oil.

7 GLUTEN FREE BAKING

Manufactured GF baked goods are readily available now but they are usually highly processed, being based on white rice flour and potato starch. They generally have a long list of additives in an attempt to replace the flavour lacking in rice and starch, as well as stabilisers to prevent crumbling. Most of the commonly available GF supermarket breads will disintegrate into a pappy mush when meeting moisture and they often have an odd taste, unless they contain a lot of seeds to disguise it. Commercially available GF flours are usually made up of the flavourless white rice flour and potato starch with added xanthum gum as a binding agent to help prevent bakes from crumbling. The result is that they contain very little fibre and have a high glycaemic index (the starches are rapidly absorbed to give you a quick blood glucose high which soon fades).

But you can make up your own mix, basing it instead on brown rice flour which still has its fibre intact. Rice flour on its own tends to impart a bit of a sandy texture and it is best used as a base to which you can add another more flavoursome flour. Most of the naturally gluten-free flours are quite strongly flavoured; the ones that are most commonly available are buckwheat, gram and almond flour. All of these have quite distinctive and strong flavours on their own so may work better when diluted a little with rice flour.

The next page gives a list of flours which are naturally gluten free and their various properties.

Rice flour (6.7% protein)is a basic inexpensive, flavourless flour; better to get brown rice flour as it contains more fibre. It produces a sandy texture in bakes so it is best to make it a background flour to other more interesting ones.

Buckwheat (13% protein) flour is now fairly widely available and is a good standby to keep in stock. It is made from the seeds of a plant related to rhubarb.

Almond flour (25% protein) or ground almonds. This is fine on its own and makes a lovely rich and moist cake but can be a bit heavy so you could substitute some of it with different flour.

Gram flour (22% protein) is made from chickpeas and also widely available now.

Quinoa flour(10% protein) is easily made by whizzing quinoa in a food processor, coffee grinder or Nutribullet, and has quite a mild flavour. It is a really useful flour to have around.

Teff flour (12.8% protein) is made from the seeds of an Ethiopian grain and tastes a little like rye. The Ethiopians make a flat bread called injera from it. Used as part of a mix it gives a wonderful flavour to breads and cakes

Cornflour is a finely ground starchy flour made from maize and is best used as a starch or for thickening sauces.

Starch in the form of potato or tapioca starch, or arrowroot is used to give bakes a lighter texture. It has no fibre and a high glycaemic index.

Oats, millet, desicated coconut, flaxseed, and other nuts or seeds can be made into flours in a food processor. They all have different properties and bring interesting flavours as well as nutritional value.

Binding agents are necessary to help replace the structure provided by gluten in wheat flours, and they will make your bakes a bit less crumbly by trapping air in much the same way that gluten does.

The two commonest binding agents that are used are Xanthum gum which is a carbohydrate produced by the bacterium *Xanthomonas campestris,* and *Psyllium* husk, which is a soluble, prebiotic fibre, from a plant of the genus

Plantago. Psyllium resembles a pale very lightweight bran and works better when ground to a powder. It forms a gel in water but will not set at high temperatures, which is why you always need to add an egg to your mix when using it. The egg albumen will set while cooking, helping to hold the structure up. Xanthum gum is sold as a fine white powder and is readily available now.

 - **Xanthum gum** Add 2 tsp to 500g flour for bread, and1/4 tsp per 200gm flour for cakes

 - **Psyllium husk** Add 18g for 500g flour for bread and 5g for 200g flour for cakes.

 Psyllium is sometimes called Ispeghula and is the ingredient of Fybogel.

CONVERTING YOUR EXISTING RECIPES TO GF

Use your usual recipe substituting weight for weight with your own flour blend or a commercial GF flour mix.

Here are some tips

 - GF flours tend to be rather more absorbent which can make the dough a bit dry. You may need to add a bit of water, or better still, a dollop of mashed ripe banana, or apple or squash puree to slacken it. - You may need a longer baking time due to the increased liquid.

 - If using your own flour mix, make sure to add some xanthum gum or psyllium to it to make the result less crumbly.

 - Use half as much again of the baking powder and bicarbonate of soda that your recipe recommends and an extra egg will help as well.

 - Whisk the butter or oil, sugar and eggs for several minutes in order to get plenty of air into it, before folding in the flour very gently so as not to lose too much of that air.

 - Dan Lepard, the baker and chef, is of the opinion that fat will inhibit the bonding of the starch particles necessary for a good rise, so he suggests using less butter and an extra egg.

- You can also substitute all or some of the fat with plain natural yoghurt. This will have the effect of increasing the protein as well as greatly reducing the fat content. You could even try arguing that a cake made like that is actually rather good for you......

> **All Doves flours** are based on starch with other flours added to give flavour. Doves Brown Bread Flour has the most interesting flavour of all of them and can be used for all baking as well as bread. It is made up from rice flour, potato and tapioca starch, gram, buckwheat and carob flours. The name bread flour is a bit misleading as in the world of wheat-flour baking, bread flour, or strong flour, refers to it being made from the hard durum wheat, high in gluten, which is grown especially for breadmaking.

BREADS

We have all got used to well-risen light breads, as over the last hundred years or so varieties of wheat have been developed to contain much more gluten. As discussed before, the breads made now also use a monoculture of yeast selected for giving a fast rise, whereas in earlier times natural yeasts were allowed to develop in the sourdough tradition of bread-making. The resultant bread was not only more flavoursome but it contained less gluten and was more digestable.

There is an interesting movement now, to return to growing the older varieties of wheat which all differ in flavour and contain less gluten. They need the slower process of the sourdough method to be at their best. If you use a Doves GF bread flour you will get a reasonably good rise due to the fact that it has a large amount of starch in it.

Experimenting with bread

By trying out more interesting flour combinations you can develop some beautiful flavours and make delicious breads. You can also decide whether you want to have a lot of starch, giving a lighter, better-risen loaf, or use a bit less starch and have a bread with more nutritional value.

- slashing the top with a sharp knife will allow the bread to rise more easily as the crust dries out.

- you will need to add psyllium husk, which expands with water to help it hold the structure, and an egg as well which helps that structure not to collapse on cooling.

Notes on gluten for the technically minded

Wheat does not strictly contain gluten but its precursors of two other protein molecules called glutenin and gliadin instead. It is only when wheat flour is mixed with water and you begin to knead it that these two molecules hook onto each other to form gluten. This new protein has long very elastic strands and the more kneading, the more gluten is formed. This makes the dough feel springy and elastic and is what is meant when bakers talk about 'developing the gluten'.

 The ingredients of any foodstuff are listed on the packet in the order of the amounts of each it contains, starting with the largest amount.

PASTRY

Without gluten, pastry tends to behave rather badly, falling to bits when it is rolled out and handled. There are ways around this and here are some tips.

- the dough needs to be a bit wetter than you would normally make it and it is even more important to keep it chilled. The resting time is particularly important as GF flours are very absorbent and the psyllium or xanthum gum also need time to soak up the liquid helping to give the dough more elasticity. A minimum of half an hour will do, but overnight in the fridge is better.

- use a beaten egg to bind the flour as well as some water.

- buckwheat and quinoa make very good flours for pastry but if you find the flavours too strong you can dilute them with some rice flour. Or just use Doves flour instead.

- roll it out between two sheets of baking parchment, or cling film if you still have any to use up, and if it still refuses to stay together, you can always just cut out discs from the dough and press them into the tin instead.

Oats contain a protein related to gluten called avenin which can cause problems similar to gluten intolerance.

8 A FEW GLUTEN FREE RECIPES

A BREAD MADE WITH YEAST

This makes a lovely dense, high protein, nutty flavoured bread, particularly good when toasted.

100g ground seeds (I use 50g each of sunflower and linseed)

375g GF flour - made up of 150g brown rice

75g teff or ground quinoa

75g buckwheat

75g potato starch or arrowroot

18g psyllium husk

7g fast dried yeast

1 tsp salt

1 tbsp treacle (optional, for flavour only)

1 tsp caraway seeds

400ml warm water

1 beaten egg

Make sure all the dry ingredients are well mixed before adding everything else. The dough will be very wet. Turn it out into a 1kg loaf tin, sprinkle a few more caraway seeds on top and some polenta, if you have any, for a crusty finish. Make cuts across the top with a sharp knife, cover and leave to rise in a warm place for 2-3 hours. It will not rise by much more than a third.

Bake for 1hour 15 mins at 180C. Allow it to go cold in the tin, as it needs to continue to dry out. You cannot therefore use the usual method of turning the loaf out and tapping it for a hollow sound to check it is cooked all the way through.

If you have a thermometer, it needs to be at least 206F in the centre.

SODA BREAD USING DOVES FLOUR

225g Doves brown bread flour

25g rolled oats

7g psyllium husk

1/2 tsp salt

1tsp bicarb of soda

a few pumpkin seeds

1 desertspoonful treacle (optional, just for flavour)

1beaten egg

170ml milk soured with 1/2 tablespoonful of lemon juice. (You can substitute buttermilk or yoghurt for the milk, in which case you will not need to add the lemon juice).

Make sure the dry ingredients are well mixed before adding the wet ingredients. The dough will be quite sticky but turn it out onto a floured surface and lightly pat it into shape before placing on a baking tray. Make two deep slashes in a cross shape through the top and bake at 200C for 40 minutes.

A bit of chemistry

It is the action of the alkali (bicarbonate of soda) with an acid that forms the bubbles of carbon dioxide that make the bread rise; buttermilk and yoghurt are already naturally acidic. If you do not have either of these then you can use one tablespoonful of lemon juice or 2 level teaspoonsful of cream of tartar per 450ml milk instead.

ANOTHER SODA BREAD

This recipe is similar to the previous one but it uses a different mix of flours and is baked in a tin.

125g buckwheat or quinoa flour

100g potato starch

7g psyllium husk

1/2 tsp salt

1tsp bicarbonate of soda

a handful of chopped walnuts

1 beaten egg

225ml milk soured with 1/2 a tablespoonful of lemon juice. Or use buttermilk or yoghurt

This will make a very wet dough which you pour into a lined small loaf tin. Bake at 200C for 50 minutes.

The increased liquid content will make it easier for the dough to rise more, and the restriction of the loaf tin will push the rise upwards making for more of a loaf shape than the scone form of traditional soda bread. Due to the added liquid content it will need longer in the oven to cook through.

FLATBREADS

200g buckwheat or quinoa flour, or a mixture of both

9g psyllium husk

1 tsp salt

250ml water

Mix together and rest for at least half an hour to hydrate the flour, then take a piece of the dough and drop it onto a floured surface. Pull off a piece the size of a small egg, shape it into a ball and roll out thinly into an oval. Brush a small frying pan with oil and bring it to medium heat before dropping the flattened piece of dough into the pan. Fry for a few minutes and then take a corner of a folded up teatowel and bounce it onto the surface of the flatbread until bubbles start to appear. Turn over and cook the other side for another minute or two.

These will keep for 3 -4 days in the fridge and can also be used as wraps.

Garbanzo is another name for the chickpea.

KNEKKEBROD or NORWEGIAN SEED CRACKERS

My thanks to Lis McLoughlin for this one

1 cup of mixed seeds. (Any combination of sunflower, pumpkin, linseed, sesame, chia or poppy seeds)

1.5 cups of rolled oats

1.5 cups buckwheat flour

a pinch of salt

optional flavouring of chopped rosemary or black pepper

Add enough water to make a squidgy dough. Line a baking tray with baking parchment and press the sticky dough onto it. Spread it as thinly as possible - if this is difficult, add some more water.

Bake for at least half an hour at 160 C. They need to dry out completely so you may need to turn over, peel the parchment away and return to the oven to dry out. Break into pieces when cool.

The cooking time will be longer the more water you have added.

GINGER OAT BISCUITS

40g butter

80g soft light brown sugar

2 tsps olive oil

1 egg

125g buckwheat flour

100g rolled oats

1 tbsp ground ginger

2 pieces of stem ginger in syrup chopped finely

1 tsp baking powder

1/4 tsp bicarbonate of soda

Cream together the butter and sugar then beat in the egg and olive oil. Mix in the rest of the ingredients.

Take a good teaspoonful of the mixture and place on a baking tray, squashing it down to a flattened disc shape using a dampened fork. These biscuits will not spread in the oven so they can be placed close together. It should make roughly 16 biscuits.

Bake at 170C for 12 - 15 minutes.

FLAPJACKS

The cocoa powder is just enough to cut through the sweetness of these flapjacks while giving just a hint of chocolate flavour.

50g butter

35g sugar

15g golden syrup

80g rolled oats

20g buckwheat flour

1 tablespoonful desicated coconut

1 tablespoonful dried cranberries

3g (one and a half teaspoonsful) cocoa powder

Melt the butter and sugars in a saucepan then stir in everything else. Press into a tin, mark out in squares with a sharp knife and bake at 170C for 25 minutes.

CARROT CAKE

A lovely moist cake, good for dessert with some fruit and cream

160g caster sugar

90ml olive oil

3 eggs

zest of an orange and 1tsp vanilla extract

2 or 3 carrots grated, roughly 200g

190g ground almonds

50g any GF flour

2tsp baking powder

Whisk the sugar, oil and eggs for several minutes to aerate well, then add the carrot, orange zest and vanilla. Fold in the dry ingredients and tip into a lined 23cm cake tin and bake at 180C for about 40 minutes until risen and springy to touch.

ANOTHER CARROT CAKE

A lighter, everyday cake, this one does not have any butter or oil but uses yoghurt instead.

180g soft brown sugar

100g natural yoghurt

3 eggs

2 - 3 carrots grated, roughly 220g

150g ground almonds

50g buckwheat flour

50g potato starch or arrowroot

1/4 tsp xanthum gum

You could substitute the buckwheat, starch and xanthum gum with 100g of Doves flour.

a good handful of chopped walnuts

2tsp baking powder

1tsp baking soda

1tsp each of cinnamon and mixed spice

2tsp ground ginger

1/2 tsp salt

The dry ingredients need to be well combined.

Whisk the sugar, yoghurt and eggs for a couple of minutes to aerate them well, then add the carrot. Fold in the dry ingredients and bake in a lined 1kg loaf or cake tin for 45 - 60minutes at 180Cuntil springy to touch and a skewer comes out clean.

PASTRY 1

This makes a reasonably pliable pastry which can be rolled out.

200g Doves GF flour (if making your own try half and half buckwheat and rice flour with 1/4 tsp xanthum gum or 5g psyllium husk)

100g butter

1 egg

Rub in the flour and fat or whizz in a food processor. Add the beaten egg and some water, if needed, to bring it all together. Rest the dough in the fridge for at least half an hour before rolling out between two pieces of cling film or baking parchment.

The psyllium makes the pastry more pliable as it holds more moisture. If you want a shorter, more crumbly pastry, then leave it out.

PASTRY 2

This makes a much shorter pastry with a delicious flavour but it is less robust than the previous one.

70g rolled oats

50g ground almonds

2 tbsp potato starch or arrowroot

pinch of salt

50g butter

1 egg

Pulse all the dry ingredients in a food processor to make a coarse flour then add the butter. Bring the dough together with the beaten egg, and a little water if necessary. Shape into a ball and rest it in the fridge for at least half an hour. Don't even attempt to roll it out, just press into a greased 20cm tin.

CELERIAC LATKES

These are delicious on their own or with with smoked fish or bacon for breakfast. Add a green salad and you have lunch.

half a small celeriac, approx 200g

1 small red onion

3 eggs

I tbsp flour

freshly ground black pepper and a little salt

a few caraway, cumin or fennel seeds (optional)

Peel the celeriac and grate it along with the red onion (it is easier to use a food processor to do this).

Beat the eggs and put in a bowl along with the grated celeriac and onion, then mix in the flour. Add the seasonings and mix well together.

Heat a non-stick frying pan with a little olive oil and drop in about a tablespoonful at a time, frying for a few minutes on each side until golden brown.

These will keep for a few days in the fridge and can be warmed up when needed.

CHARD FRITTERS

A little like individual omelettes, these are lovely for breakfast.

4 eggs beaten

1 tbsp cottage cheese or quark

a few grinds of black pepper

a handful of chopped chard or spinach

a few chopped herbs if you have them, tarragon is particularly good

Mix everything together, then heat a non-stick frying pan with a little olive oil and fry a tablespoonful at a time until set and golden in colour.

A batch of these will sit happily in the fridge for a few days and can be warmed up as needed.

RECOMMENDED READING

For more information on most of the subjects covered I can recommend the following books. Michael Moseley's book is a real page-turner.

Gut by Giulia Enders

The Clever Guts Diet by Michael Moseley

English Bread and Yeast Cookery by Elizabeth David

All the material used in this book has come from sources which I trust, and any errors in using these are mine.

ACKNOWLEDGEMENTS

I am indebted to Janine Pope for enhancing the text with her delightful illustrations and to Niki Medlik who, with her usual flair, has conjured up another brilliant cover design. To Judy Meredith and Grizelda Tyler I would like to say a huge thank you for your help with editing and proof reading. Finally to all those friends who have made it possible to get the book publicised to fulfill its purpose of raising money for the food banks in these troubling times.

I hope you have found this book useful. Any comments, corrections or contributions for a future edition are welcome.

I can be contacted through www.thebookstudio.co.uk

This page has been left blank for you to add notes

This page has been left blank for you to add notes